Ro the Robot

by Daphne Greaves
illustrated by Lance Lekander

Harcourt
SCHOOL PUBLISHERS

Printed in China

ISBN 10: 0-15-350099-9
ISBN 13: 978-0-15-350099-2

Ordering Options
ISBN 10: 0-15-349938-9 (Grade 3 ELL Collection)
ISBN 13: 978-0-15-349938-8 (Grade 3 ELL Collection)
ISBN 10: 0-15-357265-5 (package of 5)
ISBN 13: 978-0-15-357265-4 (package of 5)

1 2 3 4 5 6 7 8 9 10 985 12 11 10 09 08 07 06

Characters

| Narrator 1 | Rory | Olivia | Ava |
| Narrator 2 | John | Pablo | Tracy |

Setting: A robot contest

Narrator 1: Meet Rory.

Rory: Greetings, humans! I am a robot!

Narrator 2: Students who are in a robot club made Rory.

Narrator 1: John is president of the Robot Club.

Narrator 1: Pablo, Ava, and Tracy are members of the club.

Narrator 1: The club is at a robot contest.

John: Okay, everyone! We have to take Rory to the table where the judges are.

Rory: No problem!

Olivia: Rory sounds so funny!

Narrator 1: That's John's sister, Olivia. Olivia is in the second grade.

Narrator 2: She is at the contest because she wants to learn about robots.

Tracy: Rory can say four different things.

Pablo: Do you want to hear them?

Olivia: Yes!

Ava: I'll press his voice button.

Rory: Greetings, humans! My name is Rory.
I am a robot. No problem!

Olivia: Make him speak again!

John: No, we do not have time.

Pablo: I guess we should take Rory over to the judges' table.

Narrator 1: The team took Rory over to the judges' table.

Narrator 2: The judges want to make sure that the team has followed all the rules.

Narrator 1: Robots must be the correct size. They cannot be too big or too small.

Narrator 2: Unfortunately, Rory is too tall.

Ava: We've got to do something if we want Rory to be in the contest.

Tracy: Let's put our heads together.

John: I've got it! Rory's baseball cap is making him too tall.

Narrator 1: Rory was wearing a Truman Grammar School baseball cap.

Tracy: Let's take off his cap!

Olivia: He looks so cute in his cap.

John: Olivia, you promised you wouldn't get in the way.

Olivia: I know.

Pablo: Come on, the contest is about to start!

Narrator 2: The whole team took Rory over to the track.

Narrator 1: The track is a path that each robot has to move along.

Narrator 2: The track has turns and curves. It has high stairs for robots to climb.

Narrator 1: Robots must go along the track two times.

Narrator 2: Robots score points for how quickly they complete the track.

Olivia: Those stairs look high. Do you think you can climb them, Rory?

Narrator 1: Ava pressed Rory's voice box.

Rory: No problem! No problem! No problem!

Tracy: Oh, no. Rory's voice is stuck.

John: We have to start anyway.

Narrator 1: Rory moved along the track saying—

Rory: No problem! No problem! No problem!

Narrator 2: Then Rory stopped talking and moving.

John: Oh, no! How will we get Rory ready in time for the next walk?

Ava: We don't have much time!

Pablo: Maybe his program needs fixing.

Tracy: We don't have time to fix the entire program that makes him run.

Olivia: Maybe—

John: Olivia, you promised not to get in the way!

Pablo: Let her speak, John. Maybe she has an idea.

Olivia: I think that all that talking ran down Rory's battery. Maybe Rory just needs a new battery.

John: Let's try it.

Narrator 1: The club put in a new battery, and Rory started back up.

Rory: Greetings, humans!

John: Thanks, Olivia.

Olivia: You're welcome. Now let's get Rory back on the track!

Narrator 2: Rory finished the contest.

Narrator 1: Rory did not win the race. Thanks to Olivia, though, he came in third place!

Scaffolded Language Development

IDIOMS Remind students that some phrases do not mean exactly what the words in the phrase mean. The words together mean something different. Have students find the idioms from the word bank in the book. Talk about the meaning of each as they find it. Then read the sentences below. Have students complete the sentences with the correct idiom from the word bank.

Word Bank: put our heads together, make sure, get in the way, ran down

1. Let's _____ to build this robot.
2. We have to _____ we follow the directions.
3. Don't let your little sister _____.
4. Oh, no! We _____ the robot's battery!

Invite students to pick out one idiom and then use it in a sentence.

Science

Make a Robot Ask students to draw and label a diagram of a robot that they would like to make. Guide them in writing three things under their drawing that their robot would be able to do.

School-Home Connection
How Things Change Encourage children to talk with family members about how things have changed since they were children. Children might find out what machines we have today that family members did not have when they were children.

Word Count: 574